Medleys of Beautiful Songs

DAN COATES — POPULAR PIANO LIBRARY

Since 1976, Dan Coates has arranged thousands of popular music titles. Composers and artists such as John Williams, Burt Bacharach, and Elton John have expressed total confidence in Dan's ability to create outstanding piano arrangements that retain the essence of the original music. He has arranged everything from movie, television, and Broadway themes to chart-topping pop and rock titles. In addition to creating piano arrangements for players of all levels, Dan also composes original music for student pianists.

CONTENTS

Produced by
Alfred Music
P.O. Box 10003
Van Nuys, CA 91410-0003
alfred.com

ISBN-10: 1-4706-1493-6
ISBN-13: 978-1-4706-1493-5

Cover photo:
Sunrise in the sea: © Shutterstock.com / Jayakumar

All-Time Favorites Medley

Arranged by Dan Coates

"There Will Never Be Another You"
Lyrics by MACK GORDON
Music by HARRY WARREN

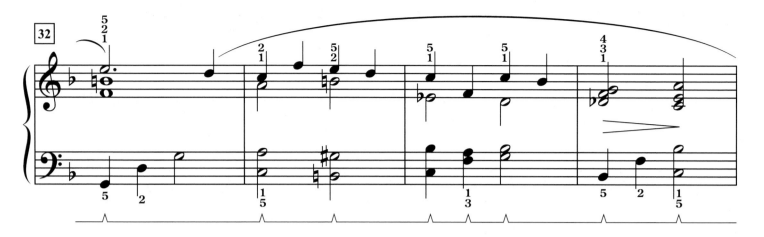

Moderately slow, with expression
"Yesterday, When I Was Young"
English Words by HERBERT KRETZMER
Music by CHARLES AZNAVOUR

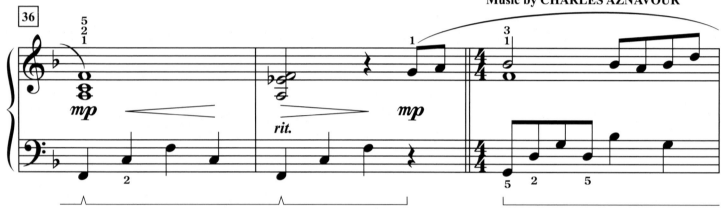

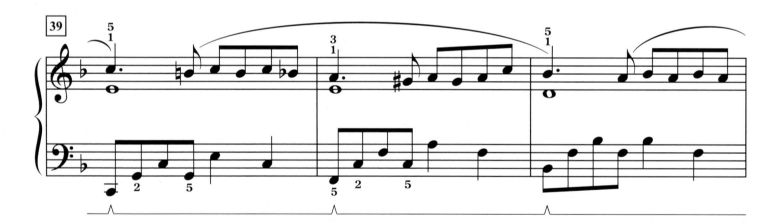

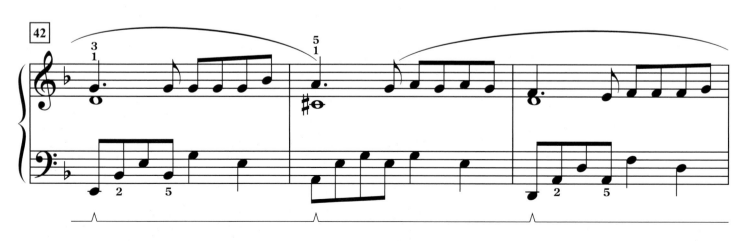

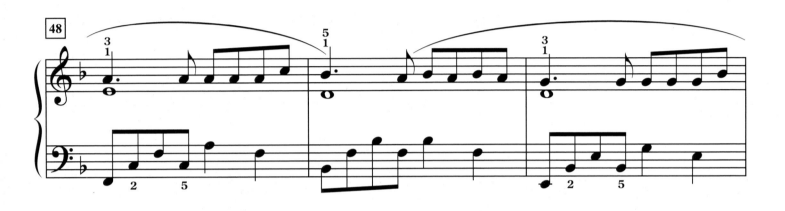

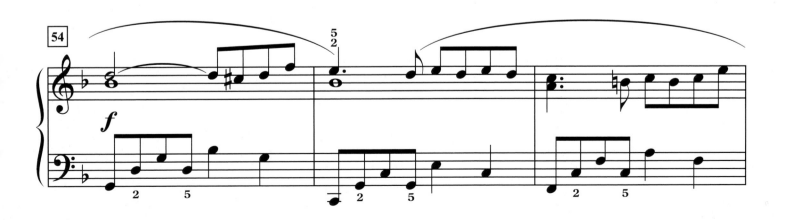

Very slowly, with feeling
"The Twelfth of Never"
Words by PAUL FRANCIS WEBSTER
Music by JERRY LIVINGSTON

Cinematic Beauty Medley

Moderately slow, with expression

"Over the Rainbow" (from *The Wizard of Oz*)
Music by HAROLD ARLEN
Lyrics by E.Y. HARBURG

Arranged by Dan Coates

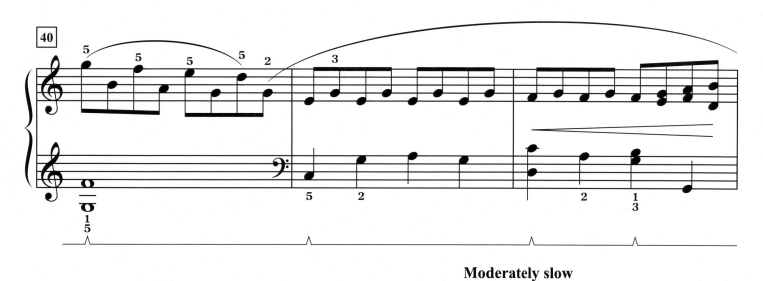

Moderately slow
"Somewhere, My Love"
(from *Dr. Zhivago*)
Music by MAURICE JARRE
Lyric by PAUL FRANCIS WEBSTER

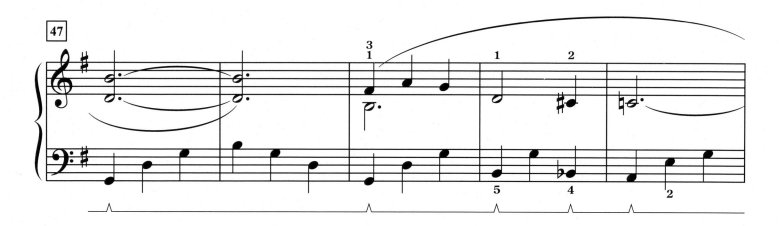

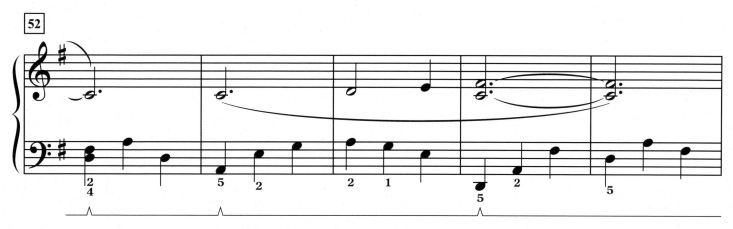

14

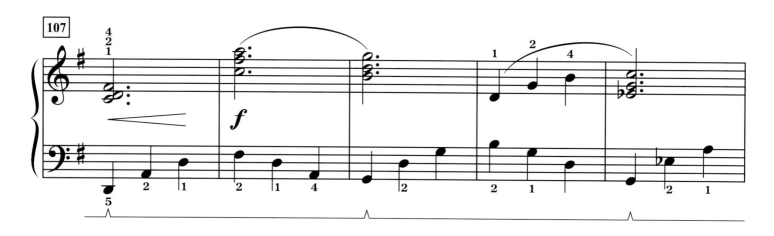

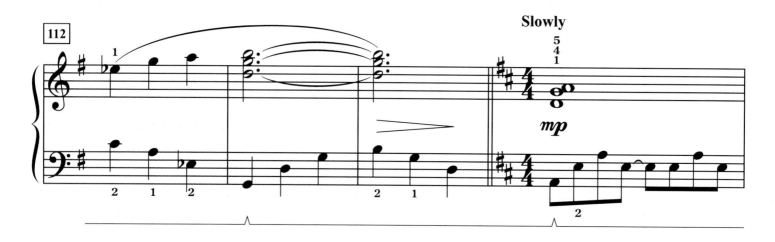

"I Don't Want to Miss a Thing" (from *Armageddon*)
Words and Music by DIANE WARREN

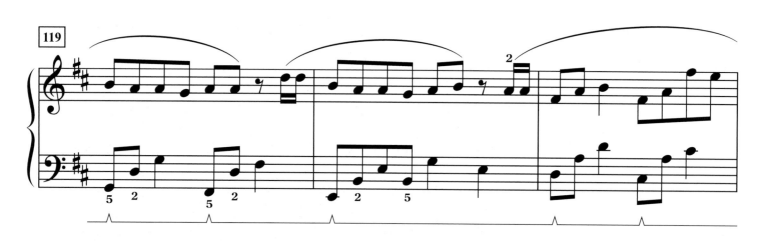

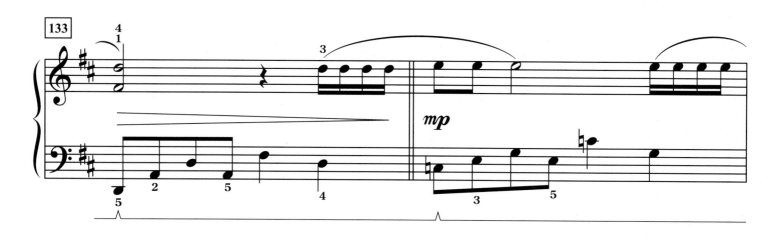

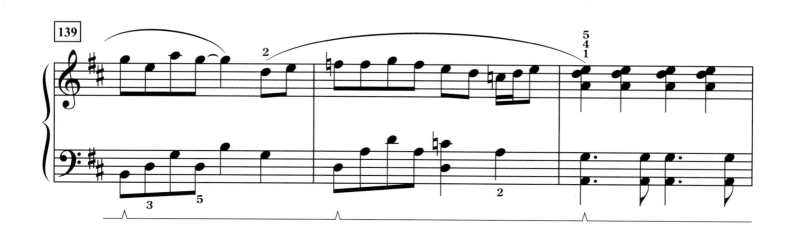

Modern Love Medley

Moderately slow
"Just Give Me a Reason"
Words and Music by NATE RUESS,
ALECIA MOORE and JEFF BHASKER

Arranged by Dan Coates

23

Slowly
"When I Was Your Man"
Words and Music by PHILIP LAWRENCE,
ANDREW WYATT, BRUNO MARS and ARI LEVINE

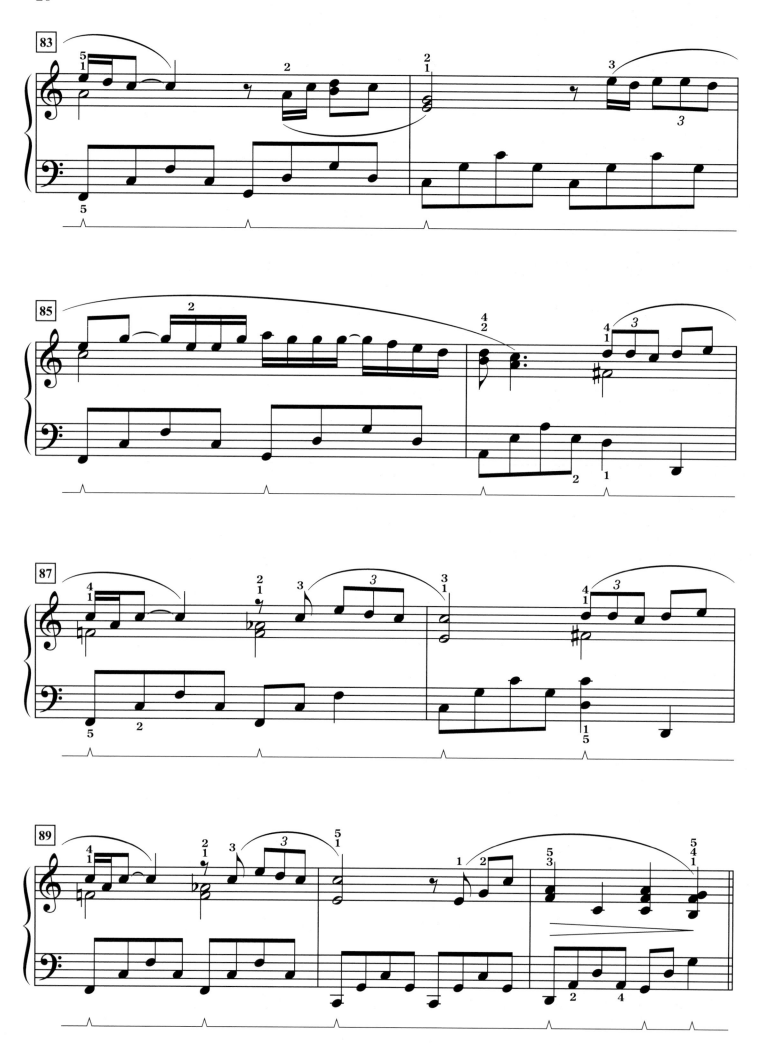

Moderately slow

"Falling Slowly" (from *Once*)
Words and Music by GLEN HANSARD and MARKETA IRGLOVA

Power Ballads Medley

Freely, with expression
"Open Arms"
Words and Music by JONATHAN CAIN and STEVE PERRY

Arranged by Dan Coates

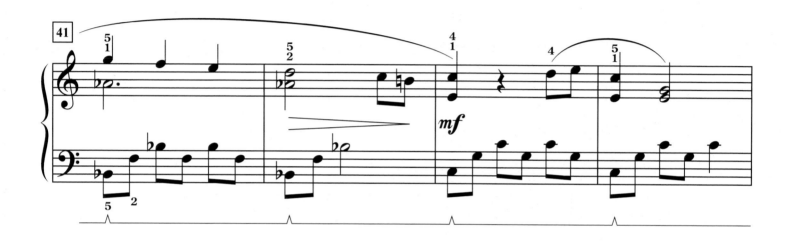

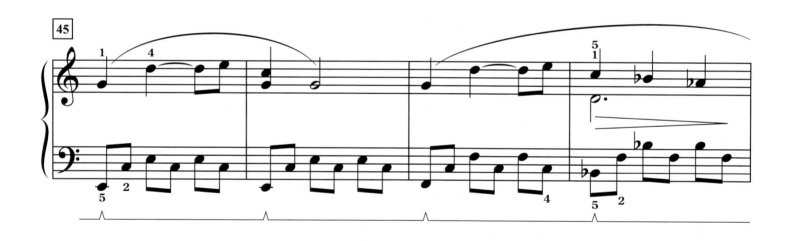

Gently, in two

"The Wind Beneath My Wings" (from *Beaches*)
Words and Music by LARRY HENLEY and JEFF SILBAR

Freely, with expression

"You Raise Me Up"
Words and Music by ROLF LOVLAND and BRENDAN GRAHAM

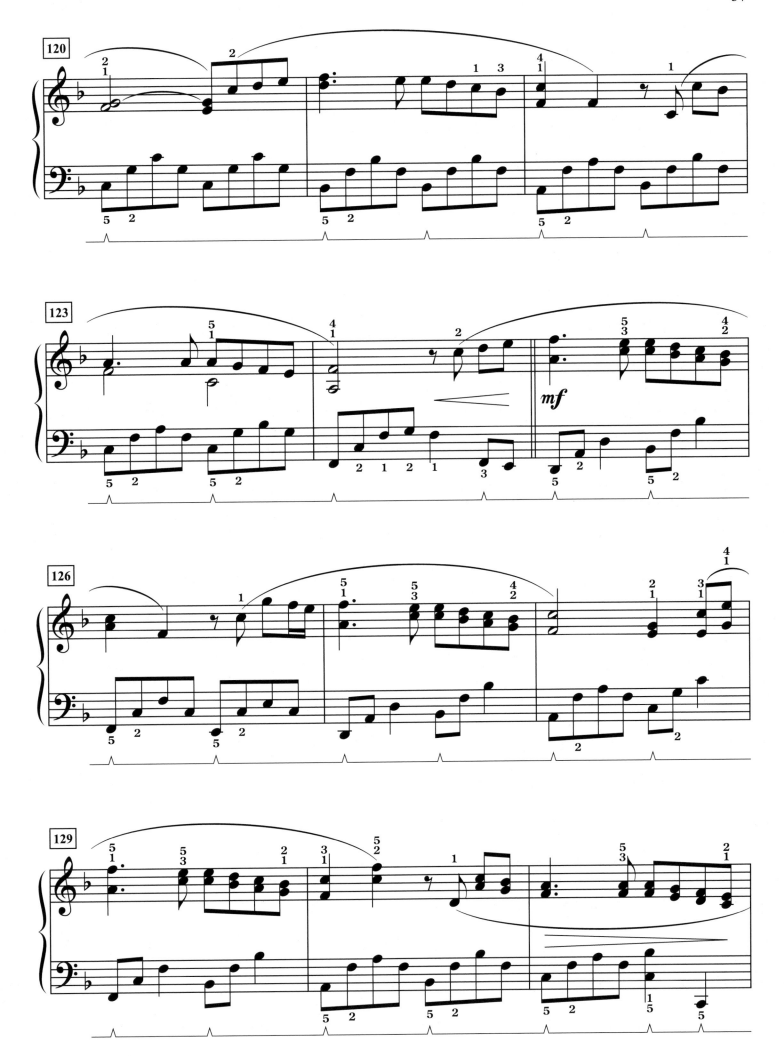

Soulful Songs Medley

"At Last"
Music by HARRY WARREN
Lyrics by MACK GORDON

Arranged by Dan Coates

Moderately slow

"Killing Me Softly with His Song"
Words and Music by CHARLES FOX and NORMAN GIMBEL

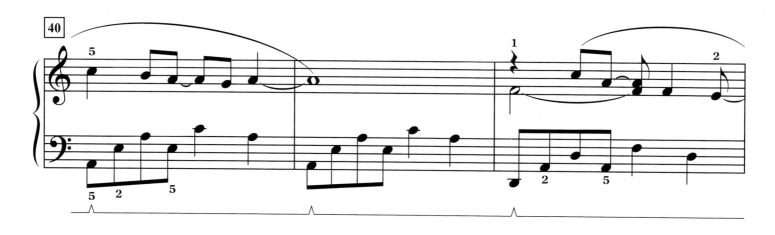

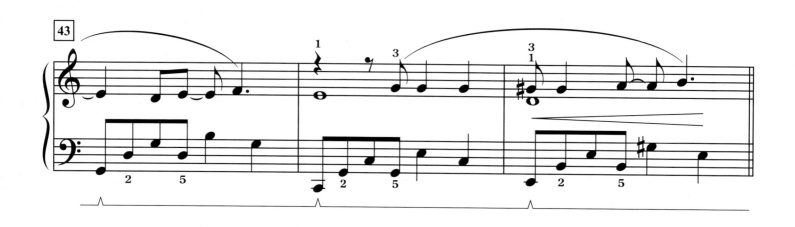

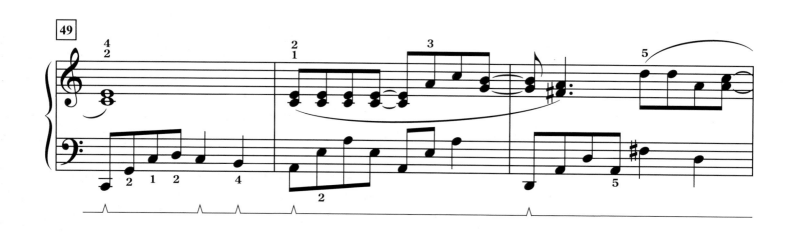

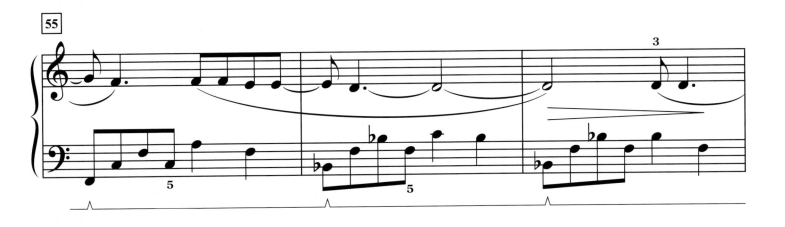

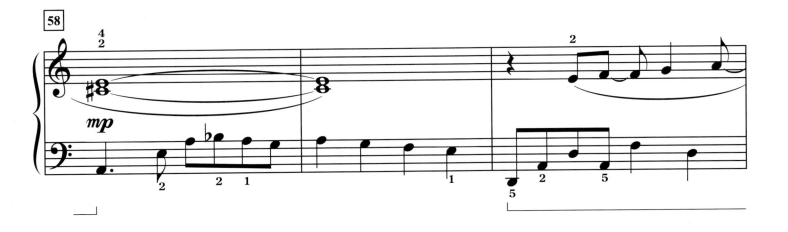

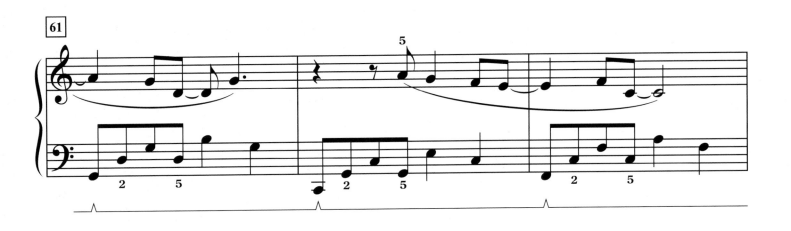

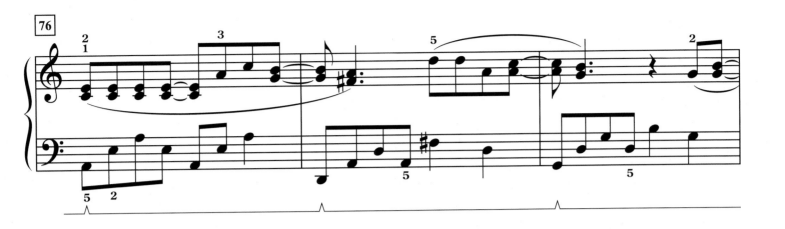

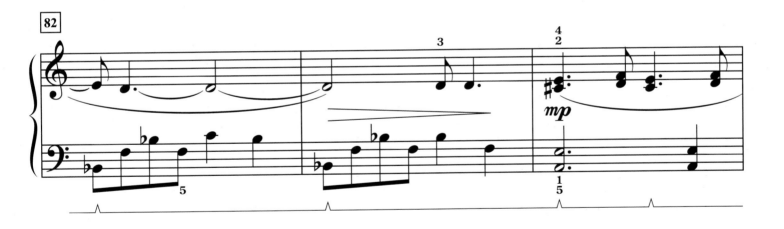

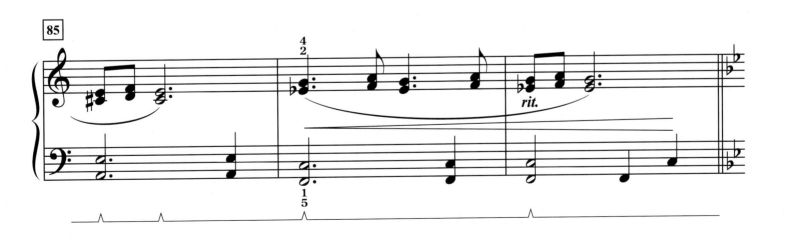

Slowly

"To Make You Feel My Love"
Words and Music by BOB DYLAN

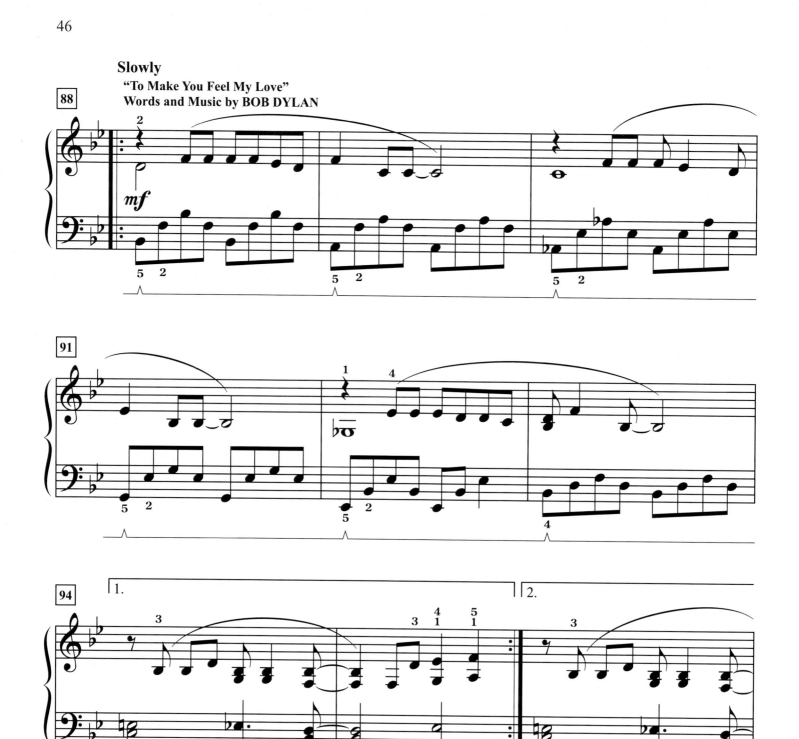

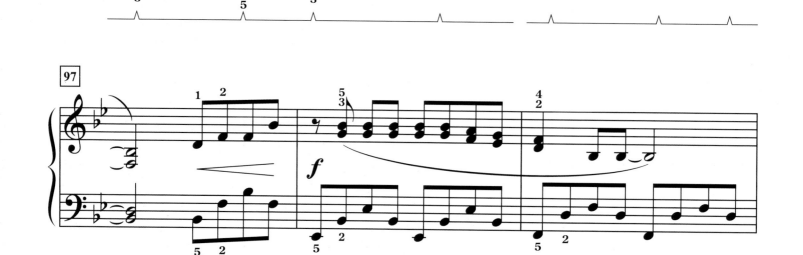

ped. simile

Timeless Romance Medley

Arranged by Dan Coates

"As Time Goes By" (from *Casablanca*)
Words and Music by HERMAN HUPFELD

Slowly
"Misty"
Words by JOHNNY BURKE
Music by ERROLL GARNER

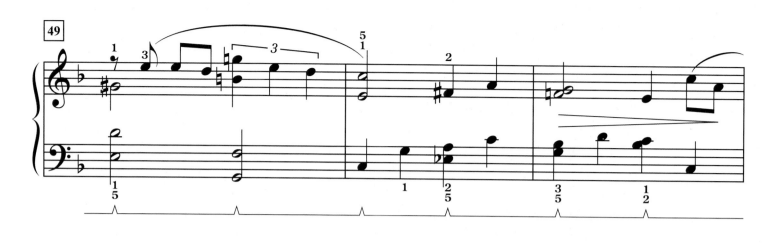

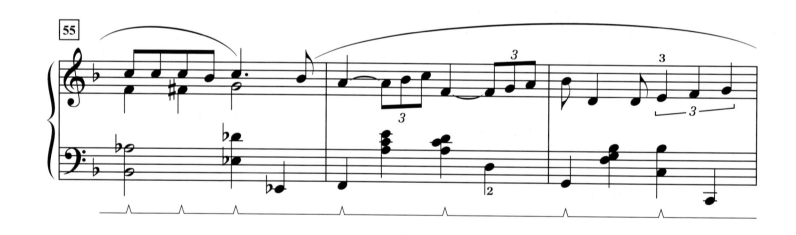

Moderately slow
"What a Wonderful World"
Words and Music by GEORGE DAVID WEISS and BOB THIELE